Dukan Recipes

40 Easy And Delicious Consolidation And Stabilization Phase Recipes For The Dukan Diet

By Sharon Stone

Table of Contents

Introduction

I want to thank you and congratulate you for downloading the book, *"40 Fantastic Dukan-Friendly Recipes"*.

This book contains information on the final stages of the Dukan Diet and plenty of recipes to (literally) get your teeth into. Many of the recipes, including soups, sides, breads and main meals are also suitable for the Cruise Phase of the diet and can help you to build a good list of meals to help you achieve your perfect weight. The last two phases of the diet are aimed at maintaining that weight and with the help of this book that should be no problem at all.

Thanks again for downloading this book, I hope you enjoy it!

Chapter 1

Eating for Weight Loss
The Last Phases of the Dukan Diet

Welcome to the final book in this series on the Dukan Diet. The first two phases of the book concentrate on initial rapid weight loss and then a slower paced, more gradual rate of weight loss to achieve your final desired, healthy weight. The third phase, the Consolidation Phase, and the fourth, the Stabilization Phase, have different aims but are both crucial parts of the plan.

Unlike other diet plans the Dukan Diet does not leave you stranded with no 'framework' for a healthy approach to food and no guidelines by which to manage your eating habits. This is where the diet differs from many others and it's why the Dukan Diet offers something a little different. Many dieters find that once they have lost the required amount of weight they gradually find it creeping back on. The last two phases of the Dukan Diet focus on a 'whole-life' approach to dieting and for this reason it has proved to be one of the most successful diets at combating the 'yo-yo' effect of weight loss and weight gain.

Breaking that cycle is the Holy Grail for many long-term dieters and the last two phases of the Dukan Diet have helped many achieve what has seemed impossible with other diets. The Consolidation Phase is designed to re-introduce the final essential food groups into your diet – starchy foods and those with higher levels of carbohydrate – but to do so at a sensible pace. The final stage, the Stabilization Phase, is actually designed to last the rest of your life. In this latter stage there are less 'rules' and more guidelines. The most significant of these is simply to maintain one Pure Protein (PP) day each week, while also committing to healthy exercise habits for life.

This book focuses on recipes that are suitable for both the Consolidation Phase and the Stabilization Phase of the diet. Many of the recipes are also suitable for the previous stage, the Cruise Phase, and some can be used on PP days (including during the Attack Phase). The book aims to help you build your repertoire of recipes for all stages of the diet but, in particular, to give you plenty of ideas for the latter two – and into the future. The book is split into three sections – "Breads, Soups and Sides" many of which can be used in the final three stages of the diet, "Main Meals", which can be used as evening meals and, in some cases for lunch, again in the different phases of the diet. There's also a "Sweets" section to make all of your meals that bit more interesting and although the focus in this book is on the last two phases of the diet, many of these can be used in the Cruise Phase as well.

The recipes in the main part of this book all contain a note at the start to identify which stage they are suitable for and, if necessary, what adaptations need to be made for different stages of the diet.

The Consolidation Phase Rules and Regulations.

By the time you reach this stage of the diet you should have achieved your desired weight. This is often where the battle really begins and maintaining that weight can be the hardest part for many people.

During the Consolidation Phase you are re-introduced to fruit, bread, cheeses and starchy products. While you no longer need to alternate PP and PV days you should have one PP day per week. It's advisable to keep this day the same each week but if, for convenience, you need to change do so over a period by moving the PP day one day at a time.

You should continue with Consolidation Phase for 5 days for every pound you have lost in the previous phases of the diet.

You can also re-introduce pork and lamb into you diet at this stage but only once a week for each. In the Consolidation

Phase the amounts of each of the new foods that are allowed are limited and these limits are:

- 1 portion of fruit per day.

- 2 pieces of wholegrain bread per day.

- 1 ½oz of cheese (hard cheeses) per day.

- 2 portions of starchy foods *per week,* pasta, rice, lentils or beans.

In addition you can have celebration two meals (meals, not days) per week. These meals can include anything that you like, from ice-cream to fries. You should remember during the meal to only have one portion of each food an no second helpings; if possible make time for these meals when you can enjoy them to their full. Also avoid having a celebration meal on consecutive days.

Remember to exercise every day – if only by walking. Avoid using lifts, and walk around the office or your workplace.

Continue to eat Oat Bran every day.

The Stabilization Phase Rules – or Guidelines.

This is the final and longterm part of the Dukan plan. It's a lifetime commitment but one that the first three phases should have adequately prepared you for. Reaching this stage is a massive achievement and you have not only lost weight but proved you can keep it off. From now on there are less rules in the diet but simply guidelines to follow to maintain that healthy weight for life. The basic rules are as follows:

- Keep one PP day per week in your schedule.

- Eat Oat Bran daily.

- Exercise regularly and consistently.

The rest of the time you are free to eat what you like – although sticking to the allowed foods lists (which are extensive by this point) is a good idea. Also focusing on low, or fat free, products is sensible, as is cooking your own food rather than relying on processed foods. This, above all, is the simplest way to stay healthy and maintain your weight.

In terms of exercise, if you feel happy to join a gym then all well and good. However, simple steps like continuing to take the stairs, walking every day, getting off the train or bus a stop early and walking to the grocery store instead of using the car are enough to help maintain the achievements you've already made.

The Dukan Plan is unique in many ways and it is designed to mimic a more traditional, healthy lifestyle and diet. By the time you have reached the Stabilization Phase you'll have adapted to many of those habits and, with the help of the following recipes, will hopefully be enjoying them (and life) to the full.

Chapter 2
Breads, Soups and Sides

The Dukan Diet doesn't mean you can't continue to enjoy added extras with your meals – including starters and desserts. When it comes to PV days there's plenty of choice and you can create some delicious soups as starters. Made in bulk, they can also allow for quick and easy options for lunch or even as a healthy, filling snack. Food in liquid form takes longer to absorb and digest and this results in you feeling much fuller, for much longer. This makes a batch of soup the perfect option for battling snack attacks during the various stages of the diet.

While bread is not re-introduced into the allowed foods list until the Consolidation Phase of the diet – and then only in limited amounts – there are alternatives. Again, these alternatives are worth knowing about and learning to make. They make lunchtime 'sandwiches' or breakfast 'toasts' feasible at all stages of the diet. Side orders of dips to go with your Dukan friendly meals area also important. These make snacking fun, after all!

Recipes

Dukan Style Flat Breads

Suitable for all Stages of the Diet, including Attack and PP days.

Ingredients

- 1/8 Teaspoon of Cream of Tartar

- 3 Eggs, separated

- 3oz of low or fat free cream cheese

Method

1. Add the cream cheese to the separated egg yolks and combine thoroughly.

2. In another bowl beat the egg whites with the cream of tartar until stiff.

3. Use a spatula to carefully fold the two mixtures together – take your time and don't let the whites break down during the process.

4. Spray a baking sheet lightly with oil and make 6 mounds from the mixture and flatten these slightly.

5. Bake at 150C for approximately 30 minutes. The finished 'bread' should be soft but not crumbly.

6. Cool on the sheet for a minute or two and then transfer to a rack to cool fully.

7. Allow to rest covered for around 20 minutes before using. These breads can also be frozen – so bulk amounts can be made.

You can make savory or sweet versions of this 'bread'. Non-fructose sweetener for sweet breads and herbs (mustard or dill) for use with burgers or breakfast recipes.

Dukan Bread

This bread can not be used in the Attack Phase or on PP days but for all other phases of the diet it's a great recipe to master – it also includes Oat Bran which is a crucial part of your daily diet throughout the different phases.

Ingredients

- 1 teaspoon of Baking Powder
- 2 tablespoons of Cornstarch
- A pinch of cream of tartar
- 4 eggs
- 6 tablespoons of Oat Bran
- A pinch of salt
- 4 tablespoons of dried, skimmed milk
- ¼ tablespoon of sweetener
- 1 teaspoon of yeast
- spices or herbs according to taste/preference

Method

1. Heat the oven to 165C
2. Separate the eggs
3. Mix all the other ingredients together in a large bowl.
4. In a separate bowl, beat the egg whites with the cream of tartar until the begin to form peaks
5. Slowly mix in the egg yolks to the whites

6. When the whites and yolks are combined, gradually mix in the dry ingredients. Mix in no more than 1 tablespoon at a time and ensure that each tablespoon is thoroughly incorporated before mixing in the next.

7. Once all the ingredients are combined, continue to mix gently for a few more minutes and the place the mixture into a lightly oiled/greased bread tin and bake for 25 minutes.

Oat Bran Crackers

These crackers are allowed at all stages of the diet and can be safely eaten on PP days. They're an absolute staple during the diet (and beyond) and can be used as snacks, lunches and sides with any meal. They can also be made in bulk, in advance and stored in an airtight tin or frozen. If making in bulk multiply the ingredients as required.

Ingredients

- 1 teaspoon of linseed oil

- a pinch of salt

- Daily allowance of Oat Bran

- Water or zero fat milk to bind

Method

1. Mix all the ingredients together to a moist but stiff consistency – add the liquid carefully to achieve this.

2. Spread the mixture on a plate to thin to medium thickness

3. Microwave for 3-4 minutes until the cracker is dry and crispy.

4. Spread the cooked cracker on a baking tray and divide into squares.

5. Bake in the oven for 10-15 minutes on a medium setting until crisp and browned.

Basic Oat Bran Galettes

This basic galette, suitable at all stages of the die and on both PV and PP days, can be made in bulk and frozen or refrigerated for up to a week and they can be used to create wraps for lunch, sides for main meals or toasted for breakfast.

Ingredients

- 2 eggs (whole or whites only)

- 3 tablespoons of oat bran

- 3 tablespoons of low or zero fat Greek yogurt

Method

1. Whisk all the ingredients together to create a smooth batter, thinning with additional yogurt if required

2. Lightly oil a non-stick frying pan

3. Pour half of the mixture into the pan and cook until golden brown on each side

4. Repeat with the second part of the mixture

Chicken and Garlic Soup

This delicious and spicy soup is suitable for all phases of the diet (with the orange peel removed) and can be used on PP days.

Ingredients

- 2 Chicken breasts with the skin removed
- 1 pint of chicken stock/broth (low fat)
- 1 tablespoon of fat free Sour Cream
- 3 Cloves of garlic
- 1 tablespoon of chopped orange peel (optional, but tasty)
- 2 tablespoons of chopped parsley
- A pinch of chili powder (optional)
- Salt and pepper to taste

Method

1. Dice the chicken breast and boil lightly in the chicken stock/broth
2. Chop the garlic, the onions and mix with herbs, spices orange and chili
3. Add the mixture to the stock/broth and cook gently on a low heat until the chicken is cooked through and the flavors combined.
4. Serve with extra sour cream and Oat Bran Crackers or Dukan Bread.

Egg Drop Soup

A light, easy to prepare soup that can be used in all phases of the diet, including PP days.

Ingredients

- 1 pint of low fat Chicken Stock/Broth
- 2 tablespoons of chopped chives
- 1 egg yolk
- 2 whole eggs
- 1/8 teaspoon of dried ginger powder
- Pinch of salt to season

Method

1. Mix the chicken stock/broth in a large saucepan, add the salt, ginger and the chives and bring to the boil.

2. In a separate bowl mix the eggs and the egg yolk together with a fork.

3. Using a spoon or fork drizzle a little of the egg mixture into the soup, the egg should cook straight away, repeat until all the egg is added.

4. Stir and simmer for 5-10 minutes and serve hot.

Minestrone Dukan Style

Suitable for VP days and all stages except the Attack Phase but note that although allowed carrots should be limited in the Cruise Phase and can omitted if necessary from this recipe until the last two phases of the diet.

Ingredients

- 2 handful of chopped cabbage
- 2 Carrots
- Several florets of cauliflower
- 2 sticks of celery
- 4 (low fat) chicken sausages
- 2 pints of (low fat) chicken stock/broth
- 2 Cloves of garlic, crushed
- 1 Leek
- A handful of mushrooms
- 1 medium onion, chopped
- 2 handfuls of spinach
- Oregano, basil and parsley
- 1 tin of chopped tomatoes
- ¾ chopped fresh tomatoes

Method

1. The vegetables above are a guide and you mix others from the allowed lists at each stage of the diet – finely dice the onions, celery and carrot.

2. Add the chopped vegetables to a pan with crushed garlic and sweat for a few minutes until softened in a large pan.

3. Once the onion is clear and soft, add the stock/broth to the pan and any remaining (chopped) vegetable with the exception of the cabbage and the spinach.

4. Bring the pan to the boil and then reduce the heat to a medium setting.

5. Slice the chicken sausages quite thinly and add them to the pan. Leave to cook gently until the vegetables are cooked to your preference (relatively crunchy to retain nutritional value). 10 minutes should be long enough.

6. About half way through the cooking time add the cabbage and then close to the end of the cooking time, the spinach.

7. Season with salt and pepper to taste and serve with chopped fresh herbs, or fat free cheese.

Basic Chicken and Vegetable Soup

Suitable on PV days (although you may want to omit the carrots in the Cruise Phase) and all but the Attack Phase of the Diet, this is a good basic soup recipe and is good to make in bulk, freeze in portions and reheat as and when required.

Ingredients

- 2 skinned Chicken Breasts

- ½ a large onion

- ¼ of a butternut squash

- 2 Carrots

- ½ Eggplant

- 1 Large clove of garlic, crushed

- Salt and pepper

- 1 ½ Liters of vegetable stock/broth

Method

1. Peel and dice the eggplant and, in a colander, sprinkle with a generous amount of salt – the salt won't stay in the finished soup so don't stint. Set aside for about 20 minutes.

2. In the meantime prepare the rest of the vegetables – dicing or chopping to your preferred size.

3. Dice the chicken breasts to roughly the same size as the other ingredients.

4. Add oil to a large saucepan and heat on a medium setting. Add the garlic and onion to soften but not brown. Add all of the other vegetables once the onion is

soft and clear. Stir gently, allowing to soften but, again, not to brown.

5. Excess liquid should now have drained from the egg plant and you can rinse this thoroughly under the tap, ensuring all of the salt is removed. Once this is completed add to the pan and stir gently for a minute or two.

6. Add the stock/broth, cover and simmer for 40-50 minutes.

7. Add the chicken and stir until the meat is cooked through, add salt and pepper to taste and serve hot.

Cream of Tomato Soup

Suitable for VP days and all stages of the diet expect the Attack, this is a lovely, warm, filling soup, ideal for dreary winter days! It can also be served cold on hot summer ones!

Ingredients

- 1 Can of tomatoes

- 3 Cloves of crushed garlic

- 1 tablespoon of cottage cheese (per serving)

- 3 slices of Turkey Ham (optional)

- 1 large onion, diced

- 1 pint of vegetable stock/broth

- 1 handful of basil (vary amount to taste)

Method

1. Prepare all of the ingredients, chopping the Turkey ham (if using) into small slices.

2. Add a dash of water to a saucepan with the onions and garlic, heating for a few minutes.

3. Add the tomatoes, crushing to as you do so, and stir in thoroughly.

4. Add the vegetable stock/broth, the sliced turkey ham and the basil, stir in well.

5. Cover and cook on a low, simmering heat for 40 minutes.

6. To serve garnish with more cottage cheese and basil.

Tzatziki

This shouldn't be used during the Attack Phase, or on PP days, as it contains cucumber. However, given the small amounts, some people may choose to do so – and although not authentically Greek you could simply substitute mint! It is suitable for PV days and all other stages of the diet – making a spicy, tasty side to use as a dip for snacking or with main meals.

Ingredients

- 1 small (or ½ a large) cucumber
- 1 clove of garlic
- 14oz of fat free Greek Yogurt
- 3 teaspoons of olive oil
- Dill, salt and pepper to season
- 1 tablespoon of cider vinegar

Method

1. Grind the cucumber and the garlic together to a thick paste.
2. Add the paste to the Greek yogurt and the cider vinegar, mixing thoroughly.
3. Add salt, pepper, dill, pepper and oil.
4. Cool in the refrigerator for 20-30 minutes before using.

Coleslaw

Easy and quick to prepare, this is the perfect snack accompaniment and side dish to many a Dukan friendly meal. It keeps well in the refrigerator but only for around 24 hours. It's fine for PV days and suitable for all but the Attack Phase of the diet - though you might want to omit carrots during the Cruise Phase.

Ingredients

- 1 cup of finely shredded cabbage.

- 4 medium carrots also shredded.

- 1 small onion chopped (optional)

- ¼ teaspoon of dried mustard

- 1 tablespoon of Dukan Mayonnaise (see recipe below).

- 1 teaspoon of non-fructose sweetener (optional)

- A dash of salt

- 4oz of fat free yogurt

- Pinch of paprika (hot, smoked or standard to taste).

Method

1. Mix all the ingredients together until thoroughly combined and toss for a few minutes.

2. Sprinkle with the paprika and serve!

Dukan Mayonnaise

Ingredients

- 3 tablespoons of low fat fromage frais or quark
- 1 tablespoon of Dijon mustard
- 1 egg yolk
- salt and pepper

Method

1. Beat the egg yolk gently in a bowl

2. Add the mustard, salt and pepper (you can also add paprika or very finely crushed garlic)

3. Add the fromage frais a small amount at a time, stirring continuously. If the mixture starts to curdle add a tiny splash of lemon juice and continue to mix carefully

4. When all the ingredients are combined you can use immediately but the mayonnaise can be kept in a sealed container in the refrigerator for several days

Mock Mash Potatoes

This recipe uses cauliflower to 'mimic' mash potato and is a great side for PV days and for the last two stages of the diet.

Ingredients

- 1 Cauliflower.

- 3 tablespoons of fat-free cream cheese.

- 1 or 2 cloves of garlic (according to taste).

- Salt and pepper to taste.

Method

1. Break the cauliflower into pieces and steam along with the garlic cloves (peeled but whole). Cook until the cauliflower is very well cooked – around 35 minutes.

2. Use cheesecloth to drain and wring the cauliflower. The more moisture you can remove, the more the texture will resemble potato.

3. In a blender whip the cauliflower, the garlic, cream cheese, salt and pepper to a creamy consistency.

Butternut Squash Soufflé

Another great PV day recipe that works for all but the Attack Phase. This savory side is suitable for a range of mains or simply as a snack lunch.

Ingredients

- 2 cups of cooked, mashed Butternut squash.

- 1 teaspoon of cinnamon.

- ½ teaspoon of nutmeg.

- 3 eggs.

- 1/3 cup of fat-free milk.

- 1/3 cup of sweetener.

- 1 teaspoon of vanilla extract.

Method

1. Heat the oven to 190C.

2. Once you've peeled and cooked the squash simply add all of the ingredients and mix really well. Cook for around 1 hour until the soufflé is set and serve straight away.

Dill and Garlic Dip

Suitable as a side at any stage of the diet, this is fresh and tasty, ideal with Oat Bran crackers or, on PV days, simply with fresh chopped vegetables.

Ingredients

- 1 tablespoon dried dill.

- ½ cup of Greek yogurt.

- 1 teaspoon of crushed garlic.

Method

1. Mix all of the ingredients thoroughly.

2. Refrigerate for 1 hour (minimum).

Tartar Sauce

A dip suitable for PV days and the later stages of the diet.

Ingredients

- 1 teaspoon of Dijon mustard.

- 1 egg yolk.

- 4 gherkins.

- ½ onion.

- 2 tablespoons of lemon juice.

- ½ cup of fat-free milk.

Method

1. Finely chop the gherkins and onion, ideally use a food mixer).

2. Warm the milk but don't boil.

3. In a separate pan, mix the egg yolk, mustard, lemon. Heat this mixture very gently until it starts to thicken.

4. Now add the milk, slowly a little at a time and stir continuously.

5. Once the milk mixture has thickened add the chopped pickles and onion, stirring in well.

6. The sauce can be served warm, or left to cool and refrigerated.

Chapter 3
Main Meals and Lunches

The great thing about the Dukan Diet is that you can eat as much as you like as long as you follow the allowed food list, remember to have one PP day per week, take a little exercise every day and add some Oat Bran to your diet. Main meals needn't be small or boring on the Dukan Diet and in this chapter you'll find plenty of recipes to keep hunger *and* boredom at bay!

Recipes

Dukan No-Carb Pizza

A great meal for the evening or to take to work for lunch. This is suitable for any PV day and works in all but the Attack Phase of the diet.

Ingredients

- 8oz of eggplant

- 4oz of fat-free Mozzarella

- herbs and seasoning to taste (oregano and basil are good)

- 2oz low-fat bacon (use turkey bacon in the Cruise Phase)

- 1 tablespoon fat-free cottage cheese

- 2 or 3 tomatoes

Method

1. Preheat the oven to 190C

2. Cut the eggplant into thin slices – using the central, largest slices for this recipe and the left-overs can be added to soup or omelet.

3. Thinly slice the tomatoes and mozzarella.

4. Spread the cottage cheese thinly onto the eggplant slices and sprinkle with herbs.

5. Top with tomato slices, mozzarella slices, and cubes of bacon (or turkey bacon).

6. Heat in the oven for approximately 10-15 minutes until the vegetables have softened and the cheese melted.

Bacon, Broccoli and Mozzarella Bake

An easy recipe to get the hang of, this can make a great main meal and left-overs can be used for snacks or lunch. Suitable on PV days and all phases of the diet except the Attack. Bacon may be substituted for Turkey bacon – particularly in the Cruise Phase.

Ingredients

- 1 ½lb of broccoli.

- 1 cup of chicken or vegetable stock/broth.

- 5oz fat-free mozzarella.

- 1 tablespoon of Italian seasoning (mix dried oregano, basil and parsley together with black pepper to make your own).

- 1 teaspoon of paprika

- 3-4oz of (turkey) bacon.

Method

1. Cut the broccoli into individual florets and boil lightly in the stock/broth – add more water if necessary. Once the broccoli has softened drain and place in a baking tray.

2. Slice the mozzarella thinly and cut the bacon into cubes.

3. Place the mozzarella over the broccoli and sprinkle with the bacon cubes.

4. Bake for 20 minutes at 180C or until the cheese begins to brown and the bacon crisp.

Chicken Strogonoff

Suitable for all but the Attack Phase this is a delicious, warming Dukan take on the traditional Russian dish.

Ingredients

- 2 large chicken breasts
- 1 chicken stock/broth cube
- 10oz of fat free crème-fraiche
- 7oz of mushrooms
- 2 medium onions, chopped
- Cumin, to taste
- Salt and pepper to taste

Method

1. Place the chopped onions into a blender until mashed, then add to a saucepan to heat lightly (don't fry or cook for long).

2. Remove the skin from the chicken breasts and dice into cubes, adding these to the onion.

3. Crumble the stock/broth cube into the pan along with pepper and stir the ingredients together.

4. Leave to cook on a low heat, covered, but check occasionally and add a dash of water if required. The meat and onion should provide most liquid for this dish but if things begin to look a little dry just add a small amount of water.

5. Add the mushrooms after about 10 minutes.

6. Once the chicken has cooked through (about 30 minutes depending on the size of the cubes) you can

add the creme-fraiche and stir in. If the dish still has a lot of liquid turn the heat off and boil some of this off (uncovered) while stirring continuously, before adding the crème.

7. Add salt and pepper to taste and serve hot.

Shish-Tawook

An easy dish to prepare this is suitable for all stages of the diet. It can be amended to include vegetables for PV days or served without on PP days. It can be frozen and reheated so this recipe allows for a bulk batch. Adjust amounts for smaller servings.

Ingredients

- 2-4lbs of Chicken breasts.

- 1 teaspoon of garlic powder.

- The juice of 1 lemon.

- 5 tablespoons of balsamic vinegar.

- 1 large onion, diced.

- 1 teaspoon of dried thyme.

- 8-16oz of fat-free yogurt.

Method

1. Mix the diced chicken with all of the ingredients, thoroughly in a baking dish, cover and marinade in the refrigerator for at least two hours. Like most marinades the longer the better and six hours is best for this dish.

2. Heat a wok to a high heat and simply stir fry the ingredients rapidly until the chicken is cooked. Add sliced vegetables to the wok near the end of cooking if using on PV days or phases other than the Attack Phase.

Turkey, Vegetable Herby Meatloaf

A great main meal and left-overs can be sliced and taken to work for lunch. This works for all phases (PV days during the Cruise Phase), excluding the Attack phase.

Ingredients

- 1 medium carrot, grated (this is allowed in the Cruise Phase but you may want to omit or substitute it).

- 1 whole egg.

- 2 tablespoons of dried Italian Herbs (oregano, basil).

- 1 Onion, chopped

- 3 cherry tomatoes, halved

- 1lb of Turkey mince

- 1 medium zucchini, grated.

Method

1. Preheat the oven to 180C

2. Combine the Turkey mince and all of the prepared vegetables and herbs, mixing thoroughly.

3. Lightly beat the egg and add to the mixture, again, ensuring it is evenly mixed in.

4. Lightly oil a bread tin and press the mixture into the tin.

5. Bake for 45 minutes, ensure the loaf is cooked through and the top browned. Serve hot, in slices or cold as a lunch.

Simple Chicken Thighs with Vegetables

This is a nice, warming, satisfying meal that works on PV days in the Cruise Phase and is also suited for the final two phases of the diet.

Ingredients

- 5- 6 Chicken thighs (boned and skinned).
- 1 Vegetable or Chicken stock/broth cube.
- 1 pint of chicken stock.
- 2-3 Cloves of garlic, crushed.
- 1 tablespoon of olive oil.
- 1 medium onion, chopped.
- 1 teaspoon of paprika.
- 1 can of chopped tomatoes.
- Pinch of thyme.
- Salt an pepper to taste.

Method

1. For simplicity buy boned and skinned thighs. Chop these to sizes to suit your tastes and crumble the stock cube, rubbing this all over the meat, in a bowl.

2. Fry the meat gently until browned in a pan and then remove and place it on a plate, keeping the pan warm.

3. Fry the chopped onion, crushed garlic in the same pan, add paprika to taste.

4. Add the chicken stock to this pan and cook for 15-20 minutes on a medium heat to allow the flavors to blend.

(Additional chopped vegetables of your choice can be added at this stage).

5. Add the tomatoes, thyme and salt and pepper to season and cook for a further five minutes.

6. Finally, add the meat back into the pan and cook on a medium heat until the meat is thoroughly done.

Basic Curry Recipe

The basic recipe here can be used in all phases of the diet but is also suited to adaptations for PV days and later stages of the diet. Simply add vegetables of your choice (or allowed ones during the Cruise Phase) at step 6 of the recipe.

Ingredients

- 2 Chicken Breasts, skinned.
- 1 teaspoon of curry powder.
- 1 teaspoon of cumin.
- ¼ teaspoon of fennel seeds.
- 1 teaspoon of Garam Marsala.
- 1 teaspoon of coriander.
- 2 cloves of garlic, crushed.
- 1 medium onion, chopped.
- Juice of 1 lemon.
- 2 tablespoons of non-fructose sweetener.
- 3 tablespoons of fat-free yogurt.
- 1 teaspoon of vegetable oil.

Method

1. Cut the chicken into 1 inch pieces

2. Dry fry all of the spices in a hot pan, don't let these burn and take them off the heat as soon as they begin to smell strongly.

3. Add a small dash of oil (in the Attack Phase) to the pan and then add the onion, giving it a good stir to coat with

the spices. To avoid burning or sticking keep stirring well.

4. After 5 minutes, when the onion has softened, add the garlic, again, keep stirring.

5. Add the lemon and the sweetener, again, stirring all of the time.

6. Now add the chicken and allow it to brown, then and the yogurt and mix everything well.

7. Turn the heat to a low-medium setting and cook for around 30 minutes. You can add more yogurt if you like a thicker sauce at this point.

8. Serve with freshly chopped coriander.

Spinach Spanish Omelet

This simple adaptation from the traditional 'Spanish Omelet' is quick and easy to prepare. It can be used as a main, lunch or snacking option and it's suitable for VP days during the Cruise Phase and for both the Consolidation and Stabilization Phases.

Ingredients

- 2 Eggs.

- 3oz of fat-free Feta.

- 8oz of fat-free Ricotta (or Cottage cheese).

- 8oz Spinach (fresh or frozen).

- ½ teaspoon of nutmeg.

- Fresh basil leaves (a good handful).

- 5 – 6 cherry tomatoes.

- Salt and pepper to taste.

Method

1. Preheat the oven to 160C

2. Mix the ricotta, eggs, spinach, nutmeg and seasoning together in a bowl.

3. Lightly oil an oven proof dish and pour the mixture into it.

4. Chop the cherry tomatoes in half and place cut side up on top of the mixture and finally crumble the Feta over the mixture.

5. Bake for 40 minutes in the oven until the mixture has set.

6. Towards the end of cooking turn the grill on and finish by grilling to brown the top for 5 minutes.

7. Serve hot, or cold in slices as a snack or lunch.

Chicken Casserole

A good main meal for the weekend or for cold, wintry days when some comfort food is required. This dish is fine for PV days (you may want to omit carrots during the Cruise Phase, although they allowed in moderation) and is ideal for the latter two stages of the diet.

Ingredients

- 1 carrot cut into large chunks.

- 2 sticks of celery cut in chunks.

- 2 Chicken breasts (thighs can also be used).

- ½ pint of chicken stock/broth.

- 2 cloves of garlic, crushed.

- 1 large onion, cut into quarters

- Thyme, salt and pepper to season.

Method

1. Preheat the oven to 170C and in the meantime brown the chicken pieces in a pan.

2. When the chicken is browned add the prepared vegetables and stir in well.

3. Prepare the stock/broth while the vegetables and chicken are cooking.

4. Place the chicken and vegetables in an oven proof dish and add the stock/broth. Cover and place in the oven and cook for 1 ½ hours.

5. Remove the lid and cook in the oven for a further 30 minutes.

6. Serve hot – with steamed vegetables and Dukan Bread to mop up the delicious gravy.

Seitan Stir Fry

Seitan is a vegetarian meat substitute made from the protein found in wheat. This dish is ideal for the last two stages of the diet and makes a easy, fast lunch or supper dish.

Ingredients

- Seitan pieces – as many or few as you like!
- 3 Bell peppers, diced.
- 3 Carrots, diced.
- 1 Leek, chopped.
- A handful of chopped mushrooms.
- Small piece of grated ginger.
- Low-salt soy sauce.
- Salt and pepper to taste.

Method

1. Heat a wok over a high heat and add a little oil.
2. Stir fry all of the ingredients together, again on a high heat.
3. Towards the end of cooking add a little water if necessary to create more sauce.
4. Serve hot!

Mousakka

Suitable for all but the Attack Phase. Lamb is not allowed in the diet until the Consolidation and Stabilization phases but in the Cruise Phase, on PV days, you can use beef, chicken or turkey.

Ingredients

- 1lb of lean meat – see above for guidelines.
- 2lbs of shredded cabbage.
- 2 medium onions, sliced.
- 6 tablespoons of oat bran.
- ¾ pint of Greek yogurt.
- 3 eggs, beaten.
- Salt and pepper to taste.

Method

1. Preheat the oven to 220C.
2. In the meantime fry the meat and the onions together in a large pan until the meat is browned and the onion softened. Add the cabbage and stir in well.
3. Add some water to the pan and cook over a medium heat until the cabbage has begun to cook.
4. In a bowl, mix the oat bran, the eggs and yogurt.
5. Place the meat, onions and cabbage into a baking dish and pour the yogurt mixture over the top.
6. Bake for 30 – 40 minutes until the Mousakka is golden brown.

Cabbage Burgers

If you have some cabbage left over from the last dish, here is a recipe to use it up! These burgers are fine for all but the Attack Phase of the diet and are quick and easy to prepare. They're equally good to eat hot, or as a cold snack.

Ingredients

- 1lb of shredded cabbage.

- 6 tablespoons of cornflour.

- 3 eggs.

- 6 tablespoons of oat bran.

- 1 onion chopped finely.

- ½ teaspoon of baking powder.

Method

1. Preheat the oven to 160C.

2. Simply mix all of the ingredients together thoroughly.

3. Place onto a baking tray or skillet in burger shapes and bake for 20 – 25 minutes until golden brown.

4. Serve with Tzatziki or Dukan mayonnaise and Dukan bread.

Pumpkin Shepherd's Pie

A fresh take on a traditional dish, this is suitable for PV days. It's another good weekend dish and should go down well with all the family, even if they're not all dieting.

Ingredients

- 1lb of lean minced meat (beef is best for this recipe).
- 3 carrots, diced.
- 2 onions, sliced.
- 8oz fresh or frozen peas.
- 1 Pumpkin.
- 1 clove of garlic, crushed.
- 1 can of chopped tomatoes.
- Basil, thyme, salt and pepper to taste.

Method

1. Preheat the oven to 150C

2. Halve the Pumpkin and remove the seeds. Place the pumpkin on a baking tray and bake for around 20-25 minutes.

3. In the meantime heat a pan to medium heat. Add the meat to brown and onions to soften. Towards the end of the cooking add the garlic and stir in well.

4. In another pan par-boil the vegetables.

5. Add the tomatoes to the meat mixture once it has browned and bring to the boil.

6. Drain the vegetables and add to the meat, along with the herbs, salt and pepper.

7. Simmer to reduce the sauce to a thick consistency.

8. Remove the pumpkin from the oven and fill with the mixture, returning to the oven to heat through for around 15-02 minutes.

9. Serve with other seasonable vegetables and/or topped with ricotta or cottage cheese.

Vegetable Lasagna

Perfect for any PV day, this is an old favorite in many households.

Ingredients

- 1 eggplant, sliced.

- 1 can of tomato sauce (check sugar and salt content).

- 1 can of whole tomatoes.

- 2 Zucchini, sliced.

- 2 cloves of garlic, chopped.

- 1 egg.

- 1lb fat-free ricotta cheese (or cottage cheese).

- 1 cup of fat-free mozzarella.

- Fresh basil to taste.

Method

1. Combine the ricotta and egg in a bowl. Add a little salt and pepper.

2. Layer the tomato sauce, whole tomatoes, eggplant, ricotta and zucchini. Repeat until the ingredients are used up.

3. Top with mozzarella and sprinkle with basil.

4. Cover and bake at 170C for 45 minutes, removing the covering for 10 minutes at the end of the cooking time.

5. It's best to allow this dish to sit for around 30 minutes in a warm place before serving to allow the Lasagna to firm up.

Chicken Sausage Fettuccine

Without the Shirataki Noodles this dish could be used during the Attack Phase and on PP days in the other stages of the diet. With them it's fine for Consolidation and Stabilization.

Ingredients

- Spicy Chicken sausage – 1 pack or 5 sausages.
- 2oz of cottage cheese.
- 1 cup of fat-free milk.
- Fresh parsley, to taste.
- 1 pack of shirataki tofu noodles.

Method

1. Remove the sausage meat from the casing and brown gently in a pan.

2. When the meat is cooked add the milk and cottage cheese.

3. Bring to boil and then reduce the heat immediately.

4. Prepare the noodles according to directions on the packaging and drain. Add to the sauce.

5. Cook over a low-medium heat until the noodles are completely cooked and the sauce has thickened.

6. Serve with the fresh parsley.

7. Note; for PV days mushrooms can be added for additional flavor and texture.

Thai Tuna Stir Fry

Another perfect dish to whip up for lunch on PV days in the Cruise, Consolidation and Stabilization phases.

Ingredients

- 2 cans of flaked Tuna.

- 2 carrots, grated.

- ¼ pint of fat-free evaporated milk.

- ½ teaspoon of coconut extract.

- A handful of snow peas, sliced (from Consolidation Phase).

- 1 packet of Shirataki Noodles.

Method

1. Prepare the noodles according to directions on the packaging.

2. Lightly fry the tuna, peas, grated carrots and then stir the mixture together over a high heat.

3. Add the coconut extract, evaporated milk and stir well.

4. Add the drained noodles to the pan and stir, cooking for a few more minutes until the sauce has thickened.

Chapter 4
Delicious Deserts

Unlike so many diets, the Dukan Diet doesn't mean that you have to skimp on sweet things. Admittedly, you may need to stock up on some non-fructose sweetener! Chocolate is one ingredient that is also not off the list in many stages of the diet. These recipes are aimed at helping you to create some desserts to go with your main meals and, if the thought of a life without muffins is worrying you, don't despair! We end this book with a couple of simple, Dukan friendly recipes for tasty muffins to get you through the day. Again, the recipes are aimed at the Consolidation and Stabilization Phases but many work in the Cruise Phase as well. Enjoy!

Recipes

Chocolate Mousse

Ingredients

- 2 tablespoons of low-fat, unsweetened cocoa powder.

- 10oz of Creme Fraiche.

- 3 eggs

- ½ oz of gelatin.

- 5 tablespoons of hot water

- 3 or 4 tablespoon of non-fructose sweetener.

Method

1. Mix the hot water and gelatin (a food mixer works best).

2. Add the cocoa powder, stirring well and then leave to cool.

3. Separate the eggs and beat the whites to form stiff peaks and then add the sweetener carefully.

4. Fold the cocoa mixture into the egg yolks gently.

5. Add the egg white mixture, again folding in gently. Once the mixture has cooled, refrigerate until firm.

Chocolate Truffles

Ingredients

- A dash of vanilla flavoring.

- 4 teaspoons of cocoa powder (low fat and unsweetened).

- 2 egg yolks.

- 1 tablespoon of fat-free yogurt.

- 5 tablespoons of skimmed, fat-free milk powder.

- 4 teaspoons of sweetener (less or more to taste).

Method

1. Mix the egg yolks, yogurt and sweetener in a bowl.

2. Gently add the milk a bit at a time and mix carefully until firm.

3. Refrigerate the mixture for a minimum of 30 minutes.

4. Form into small balls before serving and coat with cocoa powder.

Savory Pumpkin Cheesecake

Not exactly a sweet but no less delicious this is a great savory dessert and also works well as a snack for those cravings during the day.

Ingredients

- ¼ teaspoon of allspice.

- ¼ teaspoon of cinnamon.

- ¼ teaspoon of ground cloves.

- 2 tablespoons of cornflour.

- ¼ teaspoon of dried ginger.

- ¼ teaspoon of nutmeg.

- 1 tablespoon of vanilla extract.

- 2 tablespoons of non-fructose sweetener.

- 7oz of fat-free cream cheese.

- 2 eggs.

- 1 cup of mashed/pureed pumpkin.

Method

1. Preheat the oven to 150C and place 3 ramekins in a baking tray. Use a towel or paper towel to stop the ramekins sliding around in the tray. In the meantime boil a kettle of water.

2. In a food processor, blitz the pumpkin, eggs and cream cheese.

3. Add the cornflour, sweetener, and the spices, blitzing again, until thoroughly mixed. Finally add the vanilla extract and blitz again.

4. Pour the mixture into the ramekins and tap lightly (this helps bubbles rise to the surface).

5. Place the baking tray onto the middle shelf of the oven and then, carefully, pour boiling water into the tray, until it comes to the top of the ramekins.

6. Bake for 20 – 30 minutes until the middle of each dish is wobbly but the sides have set. Turn the heat off but leave in the oven for a further 30 minutes to fully set.

7. Cool on the side and then wrap each ramekin in cling-film and place in the refrigerator to chill for around two hours.

Vanilla Pudding

Ingredients

- ½ pint of fat-free skimmed milk.

- 1lb of curd or cottage cheese.

- 2 eggs

- Vanilla extract.

- 1 tablespoon of sweetener.

Method

1. Beat the eggs and then add the milk and vanilla extract, pouring the milk in gently.

2. A small bit a time beat in the curds, or cottage cheese, and mix until smooth.

3. Finally add the sweetener to taste and serve!

Quick and Easy Chocolate Dream

A very quick chocolate fix ideal for lunch or snack time.

Ingredients

- 1 tablespoon of cocoa powder (unsweetened).
- 1 individual pot of Greek yogurt.
- Daily serving of Oat Bran (optional).

Method

1. Mix the ingredients together and serve or;
2. Refrigerate for 30 minutes or more for an 'ice-cream' feel.

Chocolate Pralines

A perfect way to ward off the snack attack, these little treats should help you get through the day. They're allowed on PP days too – which means you can use them throughout the diet.

Ingredients

- 1 tablespoon of low-fat, unsweetened Cocoa powder.
- 1 egg yolk.
- 2 tablespoons of fat-free skimmed milk.
- 7 tablespoons of fat-free skimmed milk powder.
- 3 tablespoons of non-fructose sweetener.
- A few drops of vanilla extract.

Method

1. Mix the ingredients together in a bowl, adding the milk slowly.

2. Once everything is thoroughly combined simply place in an ice cube tray and leave to set for a few hours.

3. The pralines can be made in bulk and stored in the refrigerator or an airtight tin. They don't seem to last too long though!

Lemon Drizzle Muffin

Apart from during the Attack Phase, this recipe will suit the other phases of the diet. PV days only, sadly during the Cruise Phase but unrestricted after that!

Ingredients

- ½ teaspoon of baking powder.

- 2 eggs.

- Zest of 1 lemon.

- 6 tablespoons of fat-free Greek yogurt.

- 6 tablespoons of Oat bran.

- 3 tablespoons of Wheat bran.

- Non-fructose sweetener to taste.

For the Drizzle

- Juice of ½ lemon.

- ½ tablespoon of granulated sweetener.

Method

1. Preheat the oven to 180C.

2. Mix the ingredients together and then divide into 6 muffin pots.

3. Bake for 25 minutes, remove from the oven and allow to cool.

4. For the drizzle, mix ½ teaspoon of sweetener with the lemon juice. Don't allow the sweetener to dissolve completely.

5. Pierce holes in each muffin, with a cocktail stick, and squeeze a little fresh lemon over each. Now spoon the drizzle mixture over the muffins.

6. Leave to cool until a sugary crust has formed.

Goji Cherry, Rhubarb and Oat Bran Muffins.

This recipe is great for PV days during the Cruise Phase and Consolidation Phase. Once you've reached the Stabilization Phase you're free to opt for cherries instead of the Goji Berries.

Ingredients

- 10oz of sweetener.
- 2 tablespoons of baking powder.
- 1 tablespoon of cinnamon.
- 2 eggs.
- 1 cup of Goji berries.
- 5oz of Oat Bran.
- 2oz of Wheat bran.
- 7oz of cottage cheese or curds.
- 7oz of rhubarb.
- 1/3 pint of fat-free skimmed milk.
- Dash of vanilla essence.

Method

1. Preheat the oven to 180C.
2. Chop the rhubarb into small pieces (about an inch).
3. Mix all of the dry ingredients together in a bowl.
4. In a separate bowl, mix the eggs, add the milk and vanilla essence. Mix these together well before finally adding the curds or cottage cheese, again mixing in well.

5. Slowly blend the dry mixture with the wet until it forms into a paste.

6. Spoon the mixture into muffin trays or cups filling each to about a third full. Add the berries (or cherries) and rhubarb at this point and then add another layer of paste. Top with more berries and rhubarb.

7. Bake at 200C for 20 minutes and the reduce the heat to 170C for a final 15 minutes. If you use larger muffin trays the muffins may need to cook for a little longer.

8. Allow to cool for 30 minutes before serving/storing.

Conclusion

Thank you again for downloading this book!

I hope this book was able to help you to find inspiration for the Consolidation and Stabilization Phases of the Dukan Diet.

The next step is to stock up on the ingredients and get cooking!

Finally, if you enjoyed this book, please take the time to share your thoughts and post a review on Amazon. It'd be greatly appreciated!

Thank you and good luck!

CPSIA information can be obtained at www.ICGtesting.com
Printed in the USA
LVOW05s1835071114

412561LV00029B/1124/P